MOTHER COUNTRY

MOTHER COUNTRY

❋

poems by
ELANA BELL

AMERICAN POETS CONTINUUM SERIES, No. 183

BOA EDITIONS, LTD. ❋ ROCHESTER, NY ❋ 2020

First Edition
20 21 22 23 7 6 5 4 3 2 1

For information about permission to reuse any material from this book, please contact
The Permissions Company at www.permissionscompany.com or e-mail permdude@
gmail.com.

Publications by BOA Editions, Ltd.—a not-for-profit corporation under
section 501 (c) (3) of the United States Internal Revenue Code—are made
possible with funds from a variety of sources, including public funds from
the Literature Program of the National Endowment for the Arts; the New
York State Council on the Arts, a state agency; and the County of Monroe,
NY. Private funding sources include the Max and Marian Farash Charitable
Foundation; the Mary S. Mulligan Charitable Trust; the Rochester Area
Community Foundation; the Ames-Amzalak Memorial Trust in memory
of Henry Ames, Semon Amzalak, and Dan Amzalak; the LGBT Fund of
Greater Rochester; and contributions from many individuals nationwide. See Colophon
on page 84 for special individual acknowledgments.

Cover Design: Sandy Knight
Cover Art: Kate Quarfordt
Interior Design and Composition: Richard Foerster
BOA Logo: Mirko

BOA Editions books are available electronically through BookShare, an online distributor
offering Large-Print, Braille, Multimedia Audio Book, and Dyslexic formats, as well as
through e-readers that feature text to speech capabilities.

Library of Congress Cataloging-in-Publication Data
Names: Bell, Elana, 1977– author.
Title: Mother country : poems / by Elana Bell.
Description: First edition. | Rochester, NY : BOA Editions, LTD., 2020. | Series: American poets
    continuum series ; no. 183 | Summary: "Elana Bell's tender poems about motherhood, caregiving, mental
    illness, longing, infertility, childbirth, and renewal reveal the intricacies of mother-child relationships"
    — Provided by publisher.
Identifiers: LCCN 2020003040 (print) | LCCN 2020003041 (ebook) | ISBN
    9781950774197 (paperback) | ISBN 9781950774203 (ebook)
Classification: LCC PS3602.E645448 M68 2020 (print) | LCC PS3602.E645448
    (ebook) | DDC 813/.6—dc23
LC record available at https://lccn.loc.gov/2020003040
LC ebook record available at https://lccn.loc.gov/2020003041

BOA Editions, Ltd.
250 North Goodman Street, Suite 306
Rochester, NY 14607
www.boaeditions.org
A. Poulin, Jr., Founder (1938–1996)

for my mother Chana
whose name means grace

Contents

Mother Country

My mother was a dead doll   I held her
                                    hand in the land of the dead
                and did not turn away

In the land where the animals made no sound
    where the cows stood at the empty lake and wept
        dry tears and the deer waited by the long stalks of dead grass
            and everything whitened in the heat I did not
    turn away from my mother
            her eyes empty of their water

✳

My country: dark and flat like tar
    you could drown in

dark as night with no moon
    a lake with no bottom: nowhere to rest
        and full of the bones of beasts no one knows the names of

✳

The distance between our countries sang

The distance between us a song
    played on the strings of a great instrument
        we do not see but know is there

like the invisible particles that make up all matter
    even the breath
        even the breath fogging the glass behind which my mother waits

the air suspended between us: no matter the distance

What would happen if one woman told the truth about her life?
The world would split open

—Muriel Rukeyser

The Tapes

the wind is still   the garden is the mind
where bulb lies low   a snake disturbs the dirt
dark hearts and tongues exposed at the root
open all the same   red silk flaps undone
red tulips bloom: little red heads
sometimes they quiet at the sound of rain
she calls them *the tapes*   made of her
they come from her   yet they are not her
no eyes no mouths   can't switch them off
they hiss & hiss into the night
thin magnetic strips ribboning her brain

The Good Years

Each child's grief is unique. I would not trade mine for yours, would not trade the years my mother's love fell on me like soft rain and I blossomed.

I remember the moment of that first heartbreak, when I crawled into my parents' big bed, an island of love in the middle of their room. Low moans rolled from my mouth until no sound was left. Mother curled my body into hers and rocked to stop the shaking. *You're taking a mental health day,* she said. Like that I was saved. I did not have to gloss, did not have to curl and spray and hide.

There she is: pulling roast chicken from the oven or sunning on our porch in her turquoise bikini, pen in hand, or gathering a circle of women in the wet grass to dance (and I, hidden in the leaves)—

⁎

How would I remember without the bright candles in the window, lit for Sabbath, without your voice reciting the prayer which promises God in everything—*Even the butter dish? Yes. Even this piece of gum? Yes. Even—*

How would I, without the black shag carpet full of beach fleas, without Daddy's scratched guitar propped against the glass of the inherited credenza, which holds Grandpa's silver Kiddush cup and the Seder plate. Without the stacks & stacks of papers you never threw away.

If I spread them out they could fill a town. If I walk them, one at a time, like stones in a river, they become a map leading back to a time when—*O Merciful, O Forgiving God!*—the smell of chicken roasting in the oven, a piece of gum stuck to a shoe, the butter dish slipping from our hands.

＊

I had no idea what I could lose.

Ruins

As a child I loved to be found;
I slipped into the alley behind my house.
My mother called and called,
and I did not answer
until I heard the net in her voice.

The ruins are invisible from the shore,
but once you arrive you've always known.
The stones are silent.
I take a photograph to remember.
Across the island olives fall from the tree;
my window opens to the sea.

The Shed

Each time something went missing—
the photo album of my first
year, postcard from a forgotten
friend, baby teeth—mother
blamed the shed, rusting
in the center of our yard.
I imagined some insatiable monster
stored out there, feeding
on all our dark clutter.

In this second season
of her sickness, my mother
paces the length of the grass
each morning, pauses
by the shed to rattle
its neglected doors.

Miscarriage

As if to say a mistake
with the way you carried it,
like a carton of eggs
shoved at the wrong angle
into the grocery bag
or crushed by something heavy.

After the news, we wait three weeks
before I insert the pill.
Four hours later the contractions
begin and the clots come out
in the bath.

Who to blame?

These are the eggs you've been given,
Mother said.
Best to check for cracks
before you leave the store.
Once you've brought them home
they're your broken eggs
and nothing to be done.

Blackout

New York City 2003

my mother calls to tell me it's her fault
her black black thoughts the cause
of this city gone dark   each window
a blank eye in the stone   the lost bodies
below swarming hot concrete   *black as Hitler*
she whispers through the wire and the steam
rises from a grate in the street
I tell her how last night on our block
folks gave away beer & ice cream & all
the meat they couldn't cook & for the first time
in years the milky way was visible—
I did that? she asks

After the Dilation and Curettage

I float on my back
in the black ocean under a black sky
my limbs held by the salted water
the only light coming from the naked
stars above my head   I watch
the two embryos take leave
of my body   they lift
like tiny lanterns into the night
returning to their place
in the constellation

Invocation for My Unborn

little bird   little invisible
do you feel the pull of my
silent song

little bird   little beating
heart I cup my hands
to make a world for you

come come little one
yes I call for you
out loud without shame

again I open to the tide
of tiny swimmers
and pray one reaches center

I've made my heart into a bowl
for you   hungry teacher
little grower from between the worlds

I call you with all my breath
and muscle   with this body
made to fill with you

I call you from my tunneled
center my millions of eggs
any of which could be you

call with my blood river
my throat & fat hands
with cooking spoon & iron pan

little one　　little bird
I feed with my mouth
particle grown from seed

treasure　　little mystery
little all the names
I do not know

little you I cannot find
in all my folds
little second heartbeat

I swear I hear
when I stand at the shore

little all the names I've named
you in my second tongue
& all your names mean *light*

little stranger　　greedy bee
your absent wings
tickle my womb

little rib formed
from my rib
little sexless fish in dark waters

little anchor
tossed from the wooden boat
of our loving

little poem
I do not have the words for

little incantation
come come

through the sea that knows your names
through black night with its stars for eyes
through the wind & all its directions

let it blow you home

Dropping My Mother Off
at the Electro-Convulsive Therapy Ward

Do I look strange? she asks.

The other patients with their flyaway hair
and unblinking eyes wander the floor.

You look like a movie star.

The nurses suggest I get some air.
Her eyes widen as I edge toward the door,

leaving her in gloved hands, quick
for a cure.

As a girl I followed her
down any steep or muddied path.

I catch my face in the sharp fluorescence
of the bathroom mirror.

Have my dark eyes darkened?
Was that shadow there before?

Who will I follow when she is gone?

When they wheel her back to me:
faint bloom of urine on her gown.

What happened in that room
while I drank coffee just outside the door?

Mother, I've done what you would never do.
Walked you to the edge, then turned away.

Elegy for Mother, Still Living

*The Lord gives everything and charges
by taking it back.*

—Jack Gilbert

I was formed inside the body
of a woman who wanted me
as she wanted her own life,
allowed to drink the milk
made only for me.
I was given mother-love,
its bounty and its cocoon
of those first years without language.
It is right to mourn the rocky hills
of Crete where we walked, my small
hand in hers for hours. The hidden
beach where we swam naked
then baked on the fine sand. Lazy
afternoons in her lap, her thick
hand stroking my curls.
Her fingers have stiffened.
Her eyes, the eyes of an animal in pain.
I hold my mother
against the woman she is.

Dead Baby

It doesn't matter what you do. The baby is already dead. Blue-veined cheese, raw meat stew, baby dead inside of you. Go ahead: twist! jump! The baby that you grew is dead. Poor you. Thought you knew all the notes of this song—Listen: the lump of cells gathered in you will never form a tooth, its heart will never beat, its eye will not view this moon or any moon. You thought—were certain—all the tests showed two: you and—now they will do what doctors do: cut it out like a cancer.

The Swallow's Thrum

what to name the air that dips behind my neck
    it lifts   and trembles the leaves

a beat of wings   and no bird
    that sound: a daughter

her shape and voice   now I can't
    forget   I imagine—

(but it's not the same is it)—
    the childless often settle on a dog

what unspools from me collects in the porcelain bowl
    this morning the dull walled ache I know

what if nothing comes?
    the air is still   temperature of ease and time

Miracle

What else to call the way the bare branches
I'd bought at the neighborhood bodega
came back to life that winter.
I'd carried them home—dry, wrapped
in paper—stuck them in the square vase,
and, as an afterthought, filled it with water.

I don't know when I noticed the pale
pink shoots sprouting from the submerged
ends: wild, reaching roots, like ginseng, or the hair
on an old woman's chin. Then tiny green
leaves began to appear at the tips,
curling over themselves with the sheer effort
of growing.

I thought they were dead.

And now I recall being in the grip
of a darkness I did not have a name for
and didn't think I'd survive. I could try
to describe it for you now: the nights
I woke with my pulse pounding through,
the heaviness of each breath,
how the effort of being inside my body
felt like burning—

What I really want to tell you is this:
how, in the parch of that long drought,
the people I loved kept bringing me water.

Water.

Though I turned my back, and did not answer
to my name, though I flung the cup away—

Let me say it plain: I wanted to die.
But something in me, some tiny bulb
still alive under all that rotted wood,
kept drinking, kept right on drinking.

Mother

We are standing in the kitchen, the last day of my visit. In the middle of making breakfast—egg carton open, oatmeal in the measuring cup—she stops and cannot move. *What's wrong? How long has it been since you've had a shower?* I walk her to the bathroom and start the water. *Lift your hands.* I pull the tie-dyed T-shirt over her head, tug her sweatpants and then her high-waisted underwear over her belly, down her legs to a heap on the floor. I test the water. Hold her hand as she steps over the rim and close the glass door. I leave her in the steam. After, I open the towel for her, rub her dry, apply lotion to her mottled back. My fingers move between the moles, scars, the smooth stretches in slow motion. *That feels so good,* she says and lifts her arms so I can rub the deodorant stick against the fine light hair. I pick out a blue satin robe. She puts on her gold earrings. A spray of perfume. Lipstick. *Look how beautiful.*

✳

thirty-five years since you suckled at your mother's breast,
pimpled nipple in your fist—
you should have your own daughter by now

✳

I have left the teabag too long in the tea and ruined its taste.
You must not be left alone to brew too long—just enough for the perfect cup. Anymore and the mind begins to sour.

✳

It wasn't until long after she'd stopped writing that I made the connection. My mother was a *poet.* Somehow I'd missed it. I feel myself filling her shadow. Then expanding, bleeding the edges.

✳

Today I release the egg and move slow enough to feel everything. The pain in my left ovary as it drops, the pinch where the top button of my jeans meets my belly. I cannot stomach the orange, overripe, and when I bite into seed the whole thing's ruined.

Mother I run in equal parts toward you and away

✳

Over a cup of coffee watching the summer rain
a longing for mother rises in me, a sudden storm—
there is no lover I long for like that

When my husband takes my areola in his mouth
I groan with a memory I have not experienced:
I am the mother and he the hungry child

✳

This morning grief comes as a crow and settles at my window:
black feather shine, fine beak, bright eye

Three thousand miles away her forearm trembles, water
spills over the glass

✳

It is definitely spring, somewhere on the east side of Central Park, and the fuchsia tulips, which match your T-shirt, push up from the dry dirt and open toward you. It is one year since your recovery from a darkness from which there was no return but you returned, so we celebrate with a photo shoot in Central Park.

The tulips vibrate against the green. Full of fever, they show no sign they will ever fade. Who could imagine it? They look so hungry—their faces open, their bodies pitched to the light.

✳

My child will never know the mother I knew before this: the woman who stroked my forehead, not just when I was sick, who held a party when I turned sixteen to celebrate my womanhood—we made sculptures, stuck tiny objects in glass, covered them with water, sealed them with wax. Under Grandpa's prayer shawl all the girls offered their blessings.

※

I'm a mystic poet, trying to live a straight life, she'd say.

Chana you have a good heart, I said. *Stop interrupting yourself.* I was four.

※

The night she is diagnosed with Parkinson's I arrive on my lover's doorstep. I am pouring out of myself. No words for this grief so I say over & over, *I'm so sad. So sad. You will never meet my mother the way she was.*

I have met her, he insists, stroking my back. *In you.*

Born After the War

A girl. Mother named her Tree.
She grew into a sapling, into
her name. Some days, she dug
the shore alone. Her fingers
brushed the metal scrap.
She didn't flinch. A rusted
pocket watch. A photograph
in sepia, faces obscured, but something
is familiar. The chin? The brow?
A baby's shoe, leather, hand sewn.

❋

Mother never wore lipstick
or perfume or left a morsel on her plate.
Loved her daughter as she loved the new
clean American soil. Never asked
her father how they burned. Never spoke
of bone or ash or of the two dead girls.
And learned to laugh and skate
and eat ice cream.

In the Dollhouse

A wooden family. I move them around; I make them move. This is
called playing. Olga, the therapist, watches and writes notes. *Would
you like to play with the dolls?* she asks each time I come to the office.
Or maybe she says family. I keep their whispered conversations secret.
They close the bedroom door.

※

The story goes that when I was a toddler, and too young to know,
my grandmother sat me on the poolside steps. *Now you stay here and
don't move.* Then she was gone, slicing the water. Of course I followed.
When she turned back to check, my head was already under, a
bubbling flower.

She grabbed me by the hair and pulled me out. Back on the steps, her
muscled arms shook me almost out of my skin—*What did I tell you?
What did I tell you?*

Later, in the apartment, I let my plastic doll have it, held her small
shoulders and shook until her glass eyes rolled back.

I told you to stay put! I told you not to move!

※

At night, in my new brass bed, I unstack the Russian nesting dolls.
Their painted mouths don't open. Through the dark I feel my mother's
wild eye. (Once, I lived inside the slow curve of her body, ate when she
ate, slept when she slept).

Inside the hollowed stomach of each doll another and so on, until
I reach the smallest wooden seed, solid, nothing inside. Last of the
mother line.

Letter to My Son, in Utero

You are not the first.

Before you, another seed took hold,
    and every morning your father rubbed my belly
        in wonder at what she would become.

When the doctor said *no heartbeat,* the air went out of me.

    My dead baby, I thought.

They would not call it that. *Embryo embryo embryo* they said,
a padded word meant to keep me from what I knew:

    Something had lived in me its whole small life and was gone.

Forgive me for loving another before you.
Forgive me also the weight of my love for you, already heavy with death.
Forgive me. I am a Jew.

    In the middle of the celebration, I always smash the glass.

Thresholds

I do not remember the months my mother was gone,
or how long until she came back to us.

In the room, a pile of dolls.
I cannot tell you their names.
Or the color of their eyes, blinking.
Or how many hours the little girl played,
dressing them, making them speak,
her knees pressing into the carpet.

(Nobody asked, but I had a job to do).

※

In the cramped apartment, a woman crouches
beneath the kitchen table,
her fingers pressed to her lips
to keep the girls from making a sound.
I was not there but I remember.

But this is Los Angeles
and they are already safe.
The war is over.

(Haven't I written this poem before?)

Grandma Sophie's Death

We circled her bed to watch
the theatre of her body failing.
Her breath scraped the inside of the throat,
the nurses turned her over every hour.

The theatre of her body failing,
we did not turn away.
The nurses turned her over every hour.
They changed her soiled diapers like a baby.

We did not turn away
as they yanked back the cotton sheet
to change her soiled diapers like a baby;
she did not resist.

They yanked back the cotton sheet,
exposed her papery flanks.
She did not resist,
except a moan, sounds like *Mama*.

Her papery flanks exposed,
she resembled a prison camp victim,
except a moan, sounds like *Mama*,
to remind us she was ours.

She resembled a prison camp victim.
I held her stiff, dry fingers
to remind us she was ours.
The hours pressed us as they turned.

I held her stiff, dry fingers.
Aunt Frieda pulled her toes to ease the passage.
Her waxy eyes stayed shut.
The hours pressed us as they turned.

Aunt Frieda pulled her toes to ease the passage,
Mom bent to her and whispered Yiddish.
Her waxy eyes stayed shut.
The Filipino nurses tried to feed her.

Mom bent to her and whispered Yiddish,
her breath a kind of prayer.
The Filipino nurses tried to feed her,
though she could no longer swallow.

Her breath a kind of prayer,
we listened to its breaks and starts
though she could not swallow.
What else could we do?

We listened to its breaks and starts—
a startling music in the room.
What else could we do?
We circled her bed to watch

her body failing and its music.

Survival

About the night, dear one,
what does that teach you?

A woman burns bright, bright,
then crashes against the rocks.

From their wooden boats,
the fishermen watch.

A star, lighting the dark sky.
A woman falls from the roof.

The Dog

My father calls from L.A.: *The dog's dead.*
The dog (I never thought too much about)
died in his sleep, an epileptic fit.
Dad buried his ashes out by the shed,
laid his collar on top of the mantel.
It's midnight in New York, I want to sleep,
but Dad goes on about the dog until
he's done, and then a silence—steep
enough to still the roaches on my wall,
and everything he's said about the dog:
ashes, collar, his dumb and gentle
death—the blankness spreads, a frozen
sea between us, breathing like the dead.
How's mom? I ask (the fog, the fog).

In Which I Speak of the Father

Who brushed my hair each morning,
who held my small body afloat
in the Pacific as the waves rose
around us, who brought me to the ledge
over the clean, deep lake and dove.
Father, who taught me to catch
crayfish with a net, and let me stay
in the water until my lips blued.
His blood, my blood.
His sperm that broke through
the film of the egg to make me.
His mischievous eye and wild
mustache, his out of tune guitar
which he played all night in the room
as my grandmother slowly died.
Father, who will never drown,
whose joy keeps him buoyed
while we cling to him
like a raft, an oar, the immovable
trunk of the redwood.

First Intrauterine Insemination

It was not making love
but we held hands anyway
and looked into each other's
eyes and not
at the gloved hands
as the tube went in.

Alone in the cold room, I rest
with my feet in the air
and picture the light
entering my body.
I name it: *Surya*
meaning sun.

There's a storm coming.
Soon this whole city will fill
with white: a blank field.
I will go out into the morning
before the plows,
out into the thick quiet
and crouch, letting the dark
fluid spill out of me
to mark the baby
that did not come.

I will bury it like an animal.

This Time I Do Not Give It a Name

All month the blood collected
in my uterus, as if in a bowl.
It drains out slowly, staining
the hotel robe with my body's rust.

This time the blizzard does not surprise.
Through the window I watch
snow swirl and cover the tops of buildings,
the slick black street below.

Nothing is new:
not this storm
not my blood
not these words.

Requiem for a Lost Child

She waits for the ships
against a burnt sky
as she does each day.
The sea is its own story.

You watch the pull and swell
even in the dark
and think you know its secrets
until it swallows what you love.

She was different before
they whisper from behind the glass.
Meanwhile, stones move the time
and a new child is written.

It is winter.
The future falls away.
Blossoms breathe
beneath the snow.

Shelter Island

What must I brave to keep you safe?

Arm buds   heart bulge   webbed feet   tiny fingernails

You little fish
        growing inside me

This morning baby rabbits cross the road
        a robin hops onto the deck for crumbs
                the deer grows bold for the taste of grass—

We plunge our sun-flushed bodies into the sea
        and come back welted stung by jellyfish

Even a simple night under the stars:
        sore back   grass stains   sand in the cracks . . .

Soon grows up to feed on slippery fish
        the helpless baby osprey in the nest

means the end for the fat wet earthworm
           The swallow's perfect arc and dive—

The Amaryllis

Spread in its fullness:
         blood petals
             open beyond open

the stamen's yellow tip
         calling the bee to gather
               what will become honey   calling

him to the dark center:
         the part of a woman in common with the flower

which could swallow the bee
         could swallow: finger   cock   gun

from which the child's head
         and then its body
                  breaks through

My Body Belongs to You

as it has never belonged to another
                    not mother   not husband   or lover

They cut through the layers
                    to pull you out

In the dark of womb
            we made a universe
                        blood & amniotic fluid

separated nourishment from waste
                            as God separated the waters

We didn't need anything the body didn't provide
            working for us day & night   asleep   awake

                        ※

You root for the nipple
            eyes closed   head bobbing
                            on your unformed neck

make me remember my animal-ness
            Breasts leak

even when I am away from you
            & cannot hear your cry   I hear your cry

I still feel you inside
                    kicking like a neighbor

The Field

You are out behind the house, where the grasses sharpen and grow wild,
    and the bulrushes curtain the pond,

and the dragonflies—unaware of the brilliant blue of their bodies—
    crowd the stalks growing from the still water.

Here a bee, bright with the pollen he's gathered, here the air thick with
    insect song, here the wildflowers go on and on,

and you cannot see the house now, where in a few hours the family will
    gather at the wooden table to pass the platter, heavy with food,
    in the plush silence,

looking out from behind the glass into the wild of the field.

Walking up the Dirt Path Toward an Abandoned House, I Come Across Two Goats

Tails erect, small white horns buried
in coarse black hair. They are clumped
together: black goat-stones in the field.

They do not move but for the trembling
of their half open mouths. I want
to get closer. I want to tell them *no harm*—

The moment I lift my foot they scatter, gone
beyond my sight. I hear them climbing, disturbing
the brush which grows wild in these hills.

All Morning My Mother Comes to Me

as a butterfly hovering the grass
the fallen tree   soft wood rotting

in the glade a hawk feather
dropped on the path

the curled leaf in my palm
body of the squirrel bright and split

open against the blackness
of the road   the horse's head bowed

in grief   we greet each other in these
new bodies which speak and do not lie

Call Me Animal

I am in my glory

heart beat blood milk
bones : this
body my body

my opening and then
the parts no one can see
the machinery :

a glimpse :
freckled back slack belly pink
nipples   the dark hair curled

I do not care
if the curtains are open
and the neighbor catches

some days I walk
naked as a creature
through the rooms

The Bird Alarm

rings and tells me to drink water.

It sounds just like real birds, the kind I imagine
I would hear if I lived in a place with more birds than cars.

We're so intelligent; we've created machines
that sound just like the real thing: A bird

is messy and shits on the car and flies into the glass
again, to die.

We are all practicing for our deaths,
a little all the time, our cells released

in the bath, in the hair caught in the brush,
our nails lying flat in their beds.

The sounds of the birds on my phone,
which will keep chirping long after I am returned to dirt,

fools me again.
I look around the apartment to see if one's come in.

The phone chirps. I drink the water.

What Dies in Domesticity?

Her mouth: something bloody in her teeth.
She's deep in the woods they've cut away.
What is it, this thing she's longing for
shining in the Facebook posts?
She can't be satisfied. Even with a ring.
Isn't it enough—soft clothes, fresh vegetables?
Food comes in cardboard boxes or Styrofoam.
How much waste, the crawling things she kills,
neighbors knowing what she throws away. Shame.
Closed in walls, small squares of light, hard to keep
alive in city's salt, perhaps a part
she doesn't know herself by name.

After You Had Come and I Had Not

Your fingers, furious bees
hummed inside me, until
my signature wail. You crumpled,
long frame folded at the edge
of the bed, an awkward bird.

I slid behind you, lifted
heavy head onto my lap, smoothed
the bent feathers, careful
not to wake you.

There is nothing I wouldn't have given
you then, milk from my breasts, a rib,
anything to keep you there, naked,
in the half light of my room.

And I, who had never considered
children, felt the stir of fast wings
take hold in the center of me.
I did not run. Studied the rise and fall
of your chest instead, stilled by this
sudden incomparable sweetness.

Tonight

we suckle the fat raspberries
in the bowl taking time

to roll each jeweled seed over tongue
this is the closest we've come

in these early weeks since
the baby our shared delight

the fruit
filling our mouths

In the Dark Room the Son Wakes

I was the servant of two bodies,
I ate, thought, dreamed for him—
Enough.

I hear him cry and do not move
from my bed. He must learn
to be alone and bear it.

Prayer

When you are crying & I don't know why
When I cannot soothe or quiet you
When my nipples are sore & cracked from your merciless mouth
Or when you refuse the breast
When I finger the purple stretch marks
across my thighs & belly,
the loose skin
the blood vessels burst around my eyes & cheeks
& asshole
which are because you are
When I stink of puke & milk & shit
When I begin to lose my grownup words
from lack of use
When you push the cup of blended yams
I've just prepared
on the floor
for the third time this week
& it isn't an accident
because you looked right at me
before you sent it over the edge
of your highchair
When I am on my knees
before you
little ruler
begging you
to eat, to sleep, to piss in the bowl
let me remember those many nights
on my knees
praying to another god
begging for you
to come
for life to take hold
inside of me
& bloom

The Body Singular

In the sea, its edges dissolve.

When I ask if you miss me, I mean do you remember swimming
toward each other, softening in the light under the surface.

Sometimes I want it to be over.

When I eat a ripe peach, for example: the skin and then the soft
flesh between my teeth, juice dripping—

On land each small body has a name:
peach   cicada   olive   knife

It is already almost gone.
The poppy open past its season.

After Birth

I am living outside of time and space as I have known it. When I walk through my neighborhood streets in early evening with my son strapped to my chest, I watch the other people going about their tasks: returning from work or school, carrying groceries or collecting the mail. It feels as though I am watching a world to which I no longer belong.

※

My husband comes home from a day at the office and complains about how tired he is. Then swoops down to kiss and cuddle and coo the baby. He does not touch me. He does not ask how I am. Only how the baby is. How many times the baby has pooped. Spit up. Cried.

Finally he turns to me.
You don't drink enough water, he says with concern.

※

mother-hood: the cloak over my eyes, my mouth

※

Sometimes I prefer the pump to his mouth. The pump never cries. The pump never rejects my breast. Even if my supply is low.

Two of my best friends breastfeed their babies on the bright lawn of the botanical garden. Their breasts swing like globes of fruit. I pull out my small breasts and feed my son for a few short moments before he starts to cry and I pull out the bottle. My breasts fill with shame.

※

Wanting to be pregnant was about *my* experience—how empowered I would feel carrying a child, pushing it through the narrow canal. How after that I would be able to do anything. I felt beautiful with my pregnant belly. I loved when people gave up their seats on the subway. I was Earth Mother. Goddess. Bearer of new life. I read half a dozen books on giving birth. I didn't read a single one about what happens after.

When I said I wanted a child, it was in the abstract. Having a child is not abstract.

※

It is true. Sometimes I leave the baby in the rocker swing after he's started to cry, just so I can put a dish in the sink. Or pee. Or drink a glass of water.

It is true. I have thought about throwing the baby out the window. I have thought about covering its mouth, only so it stops crying for a second. So I could think.

※

I could not have known what it would feel like to hold this creature asleep on my chest, his tiny fingers hooked to my skin. His body across mine: tiny buttocks, legs curled like a frog's, the soft hair on his back and arms. And the smell of him. I am drunk on it.

※

In one dream, I have left my infant son at Barnes & Noble. When I come back he has curled up and made a nest on top of the shelves where I need a ladder to reach.

In another, I turn my back to speak to someone and when I turn back he is gone. Someone else tells me he's gone down to the river. When

I get there he's on the bank, bluish pale and not breathing, but I give him my air and he shudders back to life. I am grateful. So grateful.

※

I love to change my son's diaper. I love to watch his anus open like a tiny mouth and release the waste. I lift his meaty legs and wipe his bottom, apply the oily cream, then wrap the whole thing up in clean white cloth. It provides a sense of accomplishment that little else about mothering does.

※

Leaving the house for my six-week checkup with the midwives, I lie about how long it will take so I can stop at my favorite café and linger over a cup of coffee and a magazine, and no one expects me home.

※

Before I was a mother, I was a woman who came and went as she pleased, who took her time picking out roses, who tried on dresses she could not afford, who talked about books and ideas, whose body belonged to herself and the men she opened to, who answered to nobody, who traveled the streets of India or Bali or Cuba in search of a particular stone or delicious meal or conversation with a stranger, which would lead her to the next jewel. She strung them together and wore them like a necklace.

Before I was a mother, I was a poet. I lay in bed on Saturday mornings reading for hours. I walked through the city gardens and in the streets with no particular destination in mind. I read my poems in bars where hunger and desire flooded our mouths, where we stood up when the words sliced through our thin costumes, where we drank and danced until 2 a.m. with the workday hanging over us. There were no children there. I lived in the land of no children.

※

I find that my moods mirror my son's.

If he is delighted and gurgling I am delighted. If he is crying and inconsolable I fall into despair. This back and forth might happen ten times in a day. Everything is better when we leave the house.

✳

I walk through the garden with my son speaking aloud the names of what we see: *maple, rose, azalea.* The words sound new. Everything has a name.

✳

He has begun to babble. It sounds like water passing over stones. When I stop to listen, when I am not trying to accomplish anything else but listening, I feel as though I am the stone being washed over.

✳

Sometimes I have the feeling that he is still inside me. My belly slack, the thin pink scar where they pulled him out. My body does not belong to me. It is the now empty house of my son.

He still suckles at my empty breasts until the ghost milk comes.

✳

Motherhood offers one the opportunity to subvert the "I," the ever-hungry I. You are serving a creature entirely dependent on you with no promise of any ego reward, of *making your mark* on the world with your work.

✳

At night, before his bath, we let him roll around naked on our comforter. He shimmies and wriggles and rubs his body against the softness of it, then looks up at us and giggles with pure glee as if to say "Look at me! I have a body!"

※

I want to laugh when I see the women flounce through the streets with their big bellies bouncing and fat diamonds on their fingers and it is clear they haven't yet walked through the door of motherhood, still on the other side, where you plan your nursery and eat frozen yogurt and giggle over a snuck glass of wine and click click click on websites with baby names and baby gear, speaking sweetly to the little bundle you imagine in the beatific way of paintings, masterpieces of light; in fact you think you are the Madonna at the center of these paintings, though you would never say it, you think you know things about motherhood that no other mother knows, that you are better—you will avoid the knife and the food that keeps you fat—you will do it right. You don't yet know how cruel your body will be to bring the baby out, or after, how it will betray you with blood for weeks, how you will wish you could send the baby back, this creature who sucks and cries all night and is never satisfied, who is here to stay.

※

When it is like this: his animal mouth on me, head back, eyes closed, no sound except the catch of his breath and the swallowing. I do not know how long. It's as if we are figures in a painting. We will never leave.

Notes

The epigraph at the beginning of the collection by Muriel Rukeyser is from her poem "Käthe Kollwitz."

The epigraph in "Elegy for a Mother Still Living" is from Jack Gilbert's poem "The Lost Hotels of Paris," and also borrows the phrase "It is right to mourn . . ."

"Thresholds" is after Ocean Vuong.

"Call Me Animal" is in conversation with William Carlos Williams' "Dance Russe."

"In the Dark Room the Son Wakes" borrows the first half of the title from a line in Louise Glück's poem "The Apple Trees." The line reads, "In the dark room your son sleeps."

Acknowledgments

Grateful acknowledgment is made to the editors of the following publications in which some of these poems, some in earlier versions and with different titles, first appeared:

Adroit Journal: "Mother Country";
AGNI: "Elegy for a Mother, Still Living";
Barrow Street: "Blackout," "Mother," "First Intrauterine Insemination," "This Time I Do Not Give It a Name," "The Good Years," "The Body Singular";
Bellevue Literary Review: "The Shed";
Los Angeles Review: "In the Dollhouse";
Mom Egg Review: "Ruins";
Split This Rock (online): "Miracle";
Storyscape Journal: "Prayer";
The Wide Shore: "Invocation for My Unborn."

I am deeply grateful to the many people who made this book possible, first and foremost my parents, Chana and Phil Bell, who gave me life, who introduced me to language and music and unconditional love.

Thank you to all my mentors and teachers, especially Laure-Anne Bosselaar, whose guidance on earlier versions of these poems was essential to their becoming, and Carolyn Forché, whose workshops at the Fine Arts Center and in Greece provided the inspiration for many of these poems. Thank you to Lauren Clark, for your generous heart and sharp eyes which helped turn these poems into a cohesive collection. Shira Erlichman and April Ranger, thank you for challenging me to find the beating heart of each of these poems during our Brooklyn writing sessions. Thank you Fayre Makeig for generously providing me a space to write during the early days of motherhood.

Thank you to my dear, dear community of writers and friends and mamas, too many to name, who share in the work and make it more beautiful to be in the world, especially: Cheryl Boyce-Taylor, Adam Falkner, Aracelis

Girmay, Sabrina Hayeem-Ladani, Abena Koomson-Davis, Cate Marvin, Syreeta McFadden, Angel Nafis, Lynne Procope, Hila Ratzabi, Caroline Rothstein, Pamela Samuelson, Jon Sands, and Samantha Thornhill. I am grateful for the work of so many poets, whose work has influenced this book, especially Lucille Clifton, Kimiko Hahn, and Muriel Rukeyser.

Thank you, Kate Quarfordt, for your friendship and stunning cover image. Thank you to Peter, Ron, Sandy, and everyone at BOA Editions for giving this book a home and making it beautiful.

Thank you to my extended family, the Ferricks and the Chakrabartis, your support and encouragement means so much. Thank you to all of my students, especially from Bronx Academy of Letters, The Juilliard School and the Lincoln Square Senior Center—you make me a better writer and human being.

And finally, thank you to my husband Jai, for all of the ways you support me with your generous love, and for helping me make the most beautiful living poem: our son Surya.

About the Author

Elana Bell is the author of the poetry collection *Eyes, Stones* (LSU Press, 2012), selected by Fanny Howe as winner of the 2011 Walt Whitman Award from the Academy of American Poets. She is the recipient of grants and fellowships from the Jerome Foundation, the Edward Albee Foundation, the Brooklyn Arts Council, and the AROHO Foundation, among others. Elana was an inaugural finalist for the Freedom Plow Award for Poetry & Activism from Split This Rock, an award that recognizes and honors a poet who is doing innovative and transformative work at the intersection of poetry and social change. Elana teaches poetry to actors at The Juilliard School, and sings with the Resistance Revival Chorus, a group of women activists and musicians committed to bringing joy and song to the resistance movement. She lives with her husband and son in Brooklyn.

BOA Editions, Ltd.
American Poets Continuum Series

Colophon

BOA Editions, Ltd., a not-for-profit publisher of poetry and other literary works, fosters readership and appreciation of contemporary literature. By identifying, cultivating, and publishing both new and established poets and selecting authors of unique literary talent, BOA brings high-quality literature to the public.

Support for this effort comes from the sale of its publications, grant funding, and private donations.

✳

The publication of this book is made possible, in part, by the special support of the following individuals:

Anonymous
Jeanne Marie Beaumont
James Long Hale
Art & Pam Hatton
Sandi Henschel, *in memory of Anthony Piccione*
Melanie & Ron Martin-Dent
Joe McElveney
Dorrie Parini & Paul LaFerriere
Boo Poulin
Steven O. Russell & Phyllis Rifkin-Russell
Allan & Melanie Ulrich
William Waddell & Linda Rubel
Michael Waters & Mihaela Moscaliuc